# The Sergeant Family

Alma C. Ramnanan

Copyright © 2017 Alma C. Ramnanan

All rights reserved. No part of this publication may be reproduced, distributed, or transmitted in any form or by any means, including photocopying, recording, or other electronic or mechanical methods, without the prior written permission of the publisher, except in the case of brief quotations embodied in critical reviews and certain other noncommercial uses permitted by copyright law. For permission requests, write to the publisher, addressed "Attention: Permissions Coordinator," at the address below.

ISBN: 978-1945532-46-7

Published By Opportune Independent Publishing Company

Illustrated By Keira Laraque

Printed in the United States of America

For permission requests, write to the publisher, addressed "Attention: Permissions Coordinator" to the address below.

info@opportunepublishing.com
www. opportunepublishing.com

Once upon a time, there lived a family that was called "The Sergeant's." This family was no ordinary family. It had a Mommy Sergeant, Daddy Sergeant and Little Sergeant. They lived in a big, beautiful land called Freedom. Everyone knew they lived in peace there because they had great people that were always fighting for the Land of the Free when it got in trouble.

One day, Mommy and Daddy Sergeant received a phone call from the Great Commander. He told them, "You will have to go and defend our land from the scary Dragon King and his evil followers. Mommy and Daddy Sergeant were not afraid to fight, but they were sad because they had to leave Little Sergeant. So, they wanted to spend as much time as they could with her before they left.

One day Little Sergeant asked her grandma, "Why do Mommy and Daddy have to go to another land to take care of us?" Grandma Sergeant explained, "Little Sergeant, Mommy and Daddy, have to go there to protect you from the Dragon King and all the evil followers that want to come and fight in the "Land of the Free."

The big day had come. Mommy and Daddy Sergeant hugged Little Sergeant and told her, "We love you, and we will be back very soon." They told Grandma and Grandpa Sergeant to take care of Little Sergeant while they were away fighting for Freedom.

When they are away, Mommy and Daddy Sergeant always sent their special messenger to give Little Sergeant presents from all the different places they would visit. This special messenger was a very good friend to Little Sergeant.

He always made Little Sergeant feel special by telling her, "I have a great gift for you." At that very moment Little Sergeant, would run to receive the gift that Mommy and Daddy sent. It always contained special powers that only Little Sergeant knew how to use.

When Little Sergeant was missing her parents, she would open this magical book that was called The Rainbow Book. This book was very interesting because it granted all the promises that Mommy and Daddy Sergeant had told Little Sergeant.

One day, Little Sergeant was feeling very sad because she didn't have Mommy and Daddy Sergeant to see all the great things she was doing. So Little Sergeant opened the Rainbow Book. She saw Mommy and Daddy Sergeant working very hard so that they could come back home to her. Since it was in the Rainbow Book, it had to come true. Little Sergeant knew that one day she would be back with Mommy and Daddy Sergeant. She just had to wait a little longer.

After a few weeks later, there was a knock on the door. It was the special messenger. Little Sergeant was super excited to receive another great gift from Mommy and Daddy Sergeant, but this time it was different. The special messenger had great news to tell Little Sergeant.

The special messenger told her, "Go to the end of the rainbow, and you will find your special gift." Little Sergeant ran and ran, faster than ever before. To her surprise, she found Mommy and Daddy Sergeant waiting with open arms. She knew that Mommy and Daddy loved her very much and wanted to protect her and all the other people from the Land of the Free.

Mommy and Daddy Sergeant were very proud of Little Sergeant for being so brave while they were gone. She even protected Grandma and Grandpa Sergeant for them.

No matter how long they were gone, she remembered that Mommy and Daddy Sergeant would never stop loving her, no matter where in the world they were.

# THE END

# About The Author

## Alma Cristina Ramnanan

Life is not what it seems when one is young. Our hopes and aspirations of that time gradually hone us and make us a better person. For me, the journey was the same as others, but my experiences were quite different.

I always had a thirst for knowledge, and that led me to my favorite past time; reading. It was the sensation of freedom and tranquility that inspired me to read and pretty soon I was hooked. My interest towards Human Resources finally paved my path to Ashford University, from where I did my B.A. in Military studies and a minor in HR administration.

All this time, I had a burning desire to prove myself. I wanted to excel and be the best in what I do. Over time, I was able to develop professional standards that have helped me throughout my professional career.

My life has always been busy, and I relished that feeling. But when my daughter arrived, I was torn between my career and family. It was hard getting up in the morning and looking at my bundle of joy, knowing that we'd be apart for so many hours. It was hard juggling a job and a newborn, but as always, I was determined to succeed in the role of a mother.

Thankfully, my husband Emmanuel was there with me each step of the way, making sure I didn't break down. And we finally succeeded! We're raising our daughter, Hana, who has turned out to be the most loving person I've known. Her smiles are what keep me going even on the bleakest of days.

I would love to send a very special than you to Emmanuel and my parents, Alma and Boris Ayala. You have always been there for us and Hana each step of the way.

My interest in reading quickly turned into a passion for writing, and so I decided to add another title to my resume—Author. I have written a children's book, *The Sergeants Family*, which is based on my experience when I left on my third deployment. It was hard reliving the time I was apart from Emmanuel and Hana but with their constant support, I was able to complete my book and now it is in the process of being published.

2017 has been a great year so far. I participated in the Endeavor Games and won a gold medal in the Novice Archery Competition. My family is safe and happy, and I get the opportunity to read books to Hana every day. Can it get any better than this?

**For more information about Alma & *The Sergeants Family*, please visit:**
**www.ssgram.com**

www.ingramcontent.com/pod-product-compliance
Lightning Source LLC
Chambersburg PA
CBHW051251110526
44588CB00025B/2952